Freud and the Crisis of Our Culture

Mid-Century Essays · No: 1

Lionel Trilling

Freud
and the Crisis
of Our Culture

THE BEACON PRESS · BOSTON

Mid-Century Essays edited by Sol Stein

To

Charles Warren Everett

This essay was written as the Freud Anniversary Lecture of 1955, the fifth of the annual lectures established by the New York Psychoanalytic Institute and Society to mark the day of Freud's birth. It has been somewhat revised and expanded for publication.

L. T.

It has always been true that a chief reason for the alienation of one generation from another lies in their different understanding of what constitutes the past. In every age it must have been difficult for a man, and painful, to realize that some event which he still regarded as immediate and present in his own experience was, to a younger friend or colleague, merely a fact to be learned from a book. In our time, as we so often say, there has been an enormous acceleration in the rate at which the present is superannuated and retired as the past. The twentieth century is more than half gone, and it must sometimes seem to us that no equal period of time ever put so large a distance of change between its first and last years as this one has, or so large a difference of formative circumstance between those who were born in the early years of the period and those who were born in the middle and later years. Our belief that this is so is founded upon the nature of the political events and the social changes and the scientific developments that have taken place over this epoch. They do indeed set the early years of our century very far away from these middle years and justify the commonplaces we all utter about the bewildering speed at which we are carried down the stream of time.

Yet there are some elements of our life that have just the opposite effect. They make the early years seem very close. Among these are certain events of artistic creation. A teacher of literature, for example, cannot fail to see that there are works of literature which meant much to him when they were relatively new in his college days in the Twenties and which mean quite as much to his students now, the meaning in both cases being pretty nearly the same. Modern literature is characteristically difficult and exigent. After a modern work has been with us for a time, we are sometimes led to form a mistaken opinion of its general easy accessibility, for it has inevitably attracted imitators, and we mistake our mastery of the imitation for a mastery of the original work. But the fact is that the great artists of the early years of the century are still almost as new in their strangeness and difficulty as when they first appeared. In literature, to speak only of that art, the work of Joyce is as difficult and momentous to my students as it was to me; the work of Lawrence is as startling to them as to me; and the same is to be said of the work of Eliot, of Proust, of Kafka, of almost every name in the pantheon of modern letters. The students, of course, do not see *quite* the same object their teacher saw, they do not have the same way of being startled and impressed. Yet they are under the same influence. To the students, the work of art is almost as new and unsolved as it was to their teacher thirty years ago. When we think of what dominates and challenges our present consciousness of literature, we see that it is the literary creation, the literary ideas, of the men of the early years of the century.

Other events of our history also have the effect of bringing the past very close. Among these the work of Sigmund Freud is especially notable. We have entered the hundredth year since Freud was born. It scarcely seems possible. It is sixty years since Freud published, with Joseph Breuer, the *Studies in Hysteria,* fifty-five years since he published the *Interpretation of Dreams.* Can it really be that long ago?

In many respects, of course, Freud's ideas have established themselves very firmly in our culture. It is not only that the modern practice of psychiatry is chiefly based upon them. They have had a decisive influence upon our theories of education and of child-rearing. They are of prime importance to anthropology, to sociology, to literary criticism; even theology must take account of them. We may say that they have become an integral part of our modern intellectual apparatus.

Yet no one who speaks of the establishment of Freud's ideas can fail to be aware of the fact that they are still very new ideas. If they have become part of what we might call the slang of our culture, it is also true of them that they are ideas which, taken at first hand, seem very startling, very radical, calling for instinctive resistance. How seldom they are taken at first hand, from Freud's own exposition of them! How easily they are misunderstood—how *strategically* they are misunderstood! There is scarcely a play on Broadway that does not make use of some version of some Freudian idea, which the audience can be counted on to comprehend. Yet when we go back to the works in which Freud sets forth his ideas, we are confronted again by their original force and difficulty, by their original aggressive novelty. We know that we have not yet begun to comprehend what they have discovered.

It is not, of course, an accident that literature and psychoanalysis should be at one in the effect they have of foreshortening history, of confusing our perspective of time by making it seem that the early years of the century, which political events and social changes and scientific advances set at a great distance, are in fact very near to us. The connection between psychoanalysis and literature is of a peculiar intimacy. It is this connection that I mean to talk about, specifically the connection between Freud's ideas and certain literary ideas of an ancient and continuing kind. I shall talk about this connection by way of prelude, as it were, to a consideration of Freud's conception of culture, using that word not in the old sense in which Matthew Arnold used it, to mean a certain kind of training of the individual mind, but in the contemporary sense in which the social scientists use it. And from what may be said of Freud's view of culture I shall attempt to draw some inferences about the cultural situation of our country.

The important place which literature had in Freud's mental life and the strength of the feeling with which he regarded literature are well known. Dr. Ernst Kris, in his introduction to the letters which Freud wrote to Wilhelm Fliess, speaks of Freud's scientific interest as being "based on a firm foundation of the humanities." This is of course true, and it is one of the remarkable things about Freud. It is the more remarkable when we consider the nature of his scientific training, which was uncompromising in its materialism, and the force of the scientific ethos of his day, to which Freud himself enthusiastically subscribed.

We must, of course, keep it in mind that only a relatively few years earlier in the nineteenth century it had not been at all remarkable to base one's scientific interests on the humanities. This earlier attitude is represented to us in a convenient and accurate way by the figure of Goethe. We all know what store Goethe set by his own scientific researches, and we know what part Goethe's famous essay on Nature played not only in the life of Freud but also in the lives of many other scientists of the century. Goethe, of course, was in the tradition of the *philosophes* and the Encyclopedists, who were preponderantly men of letters: the science of the late seventeenth century and the eighteenth century moved on a tide of literary enthusiasm and literary formulation.

Yet by the middle of the nineteenth century the separation between science and literature becomes complete, and an anatagonism develops between them, and while it is indeed true that Freud based his scientific interests on the humanities, he is, above all else, a scientist. He was reared in the ethos of the nineteenth-century physical sciences, which was as rigorous and as jealous as a professional ethos can possibly be, and he found in that ethos the heroism which he always looked for in men, in groups, and in himself. He did not set out with the intention of becoming a humanist or of finding support for his scientific ideas in whatever authority humanism might have. And if, when we have examined his achievement, we cannot fail to pronounce him one of the very greatest of humanistic minds, we yet cannot say of him that he was in the least a literary mind.

A generation ago, literary men claimed Freud for their own, for reasons that are obvious enough, but nowadays it is not the tendency of literary men to continue that claim. The belief, which is now to be observed in some literary quarters, that Freud's science is hostile to the spirit of literature, is as unconsidered a notion as the former belief that psychoanalysis was a sort of literary invention. Yet it is certainly true that, whatever natural affinity we see between Freud and literature, however great a contribution to the understanding of literature we judge him to have made, it must seem to a literary man that Freud sees literature not from within but from without. The great contribution he has made to our understanding of literature does not arise from what he says about literature, but from what he says about the nature of the human mind: he showed us that poetry is indigenous to the very constitution of the mind; he saw the mind as being, in the greater part of its tendency, exactly a poetry-making faculty. When he speaks about literature itself, he is sometimes right and sometimes wrong. And sometimes, when he is wrong, his mistakes are more useful than literary men are willing to perceive. But he is always, I think, outside the process of literature. Much as he responds to the product, he does not really imagine the process. He does not have what we call the *feel* of the thing.

Freud was a scientist—this was the name he cherished and sought to deserve. Nowadays some of us have fallen into the habit of saying that there is no real difference between the mind of the scientist and the mind of the artist. We are all dismayed at the separateness and specialness of the disciplines of the mind, and when we meet together at conferences and round-tables designed to overcome this bad situation, we find it in our hearts to say to each other that we have everything in common, very little in difference. This is laudable in its motive, and no doubt it is true enough under some sufficiently large aspect. Yet in practical fact the difference is real and important, as of course we know. The reason I am insisting on the difference between the mind of the scientist and the mind of the literary man, and on Freud's being a scientist, is, obviously, that the recognition of this makes so much more interesting and significant the relation of Freud to humane letters.

The canon of Freud's work is large and complex. The tradition of humane letters is patently not to be encompassed. I must therefore be hopelessly crude and summary in any attempt to suggest the connection between the two. Literature is not a unitary thing, and there is probably no such single entity as *the* literary mind. But I shall assume that literature is what it is not, a unity, and I shall deal with it in those of its aspects in which that assumption does not immediately appear to be absurd, in which it is not wholly impossible to say that literature "is" or "does" this or that.

The first thing that occurs to me to say about literature, as I consider it in the relation in which Freud stands to it, is that literature is dedicated to the conception of the self. This is a very simple thing to say, simple perhaps to the point of dullness. But it becomes more complicated when we perceive how much of an achievement this conception is, how far it may be in advance of what society, or the general culture, can conceive. Tolstoi tells the story of the countess who wept buckets at a play while her coachman sat on the box of her waiting carriage, perishing of the cold through the long hours of the performance. This may stand for the discrepancy between what literature conceives of the self and what society, or the general culture, conceives. At the behest of literature, and with its help, the countess is able to imagine the selfhood of others, no doubt through the process of identification; she is not able, of herself, to realize the selfhood of her own servant. What the *Iliad* conceives in the way of selfhood is far beyond what could be conceived by the culture in which it was written. *The Trojan Women* of Euripides must sometimes seem unendurable, so intense is the realization of the selfhood of others in pain that it forces upon us. Yet it is possible that *The Trojan Women* was being composed at the very moment that Athens was infamously carrying out its reprisal against the city of Melos for wishing to remain neutral in the Peloponnesian War, slaughtering the men of the city and enslaving the women and children, doing this not in the passion of battle but, like the Greek princes of *The Trojan Women*, in the horrible deliberateness of policy. Thucydides understood the hideousness of the deed, and it is thought by some modern scholars that he conceived his History in the form of a tragedy in which the downfall of Athens is the consequence of her sin at Melos;

but Thucydides does not record any party of opposition to the Melian decision or any revulsion among his fellow-countrymen. In almost every developed society, literature is able to conceive of the self, and the selfhood of others, far more intensely than the general culture ever can.

One of the best-known tags of literary criticism is Coleridge's phrase, "the willing suspension of disbelief." Coleridge says that the willing suspension of disbelief "constitute poetic faith." I suppose that we might say that it constitutes scientific faith too, or scientific method. Once we get beyond the notion that science is, as we used to be told it was, "organized common sense," and have come to understand that science is organized improbability, or organized phantasy, we begin to see that the willing suspension of disbelief is an essential part of scientific thought. And certainly the willing suspension of disbelief constitutes moral faith—the essence of the moral life would seem to consist in doing that most difficult thing in the world, making a willing suspension of disbelief in the selfhood of someone else. This Freud was able to do in a most extraordinary way, and not by the mere impulse of his temperament, for he was not, I imagine, what we ordinarily think of as a sympathetic man, but systematically, as an element of his science. We recall, for instance, that dramatic moment in the development of psychoanalysis when Freud accepted as literally true the stories told him by so many of his early patients, of their having been, as children, sexually seduced or assaulted by adults, often by their own parents. We know how his patients rewarded his credulity—scarcely any of them were telling the truth. They had betrayed Freud into constructing an hypothesis on the basis of their stories. Hypotheses are precious things and this one now had to be abandoned, and so Freud had reason to think very harshly of his patients if he wished to. But he did not blame them, he did not say they were lying—he willingly suspended his disbelief in their phantasies, which they themselves believed, and taught himself how to find the truth that was really in them.

It is hard to know whether to describe this incident as a triumph of the scientific imagination and its method or as the moral triumph of an impatient and even censorious man in whom the intention of therapy and discovery was stronger than the impulse to blame. But in whatever terms we choose to praise it, it has been established in the system of psychoanalytical therapy. From it followed the willing suspension of disbelief in the semantic value of dreams, and the willing suspension of disbelief in the concept of mind, which all well-trained neurologists and psychiatrists of Vienna knew to be but a chimera. Freud's acceptance of the phantasies of his early patients, his conclusion that their untruths had a meaning, a purpose, and even a value, was the suspension of disbelief in the selfhood of these patients. Its analogue is not, I think, the religious virtue of Charity, but something in which the intelligence plays a greater part. We must be reminded of that particular kind of understanding, that particular exercise of the literary intelligence by which we judge adversely the deeds of Achilles, but not Achilles himself, by which we do not blame Macbeth, nor even, to mention the hero and heroine of Freud's favorite English poem, Adam and Eve, who, because they are the primal parents, we naturally want to blame for everything.

If we go on with our gross summary comparison of literature and psychoanalysis, we can say that they are also similar in this respect, that it is of the essence of both to represent the opposition between two principles, those that Freud called the reality principle and the pleasure principle. Whenever Freud goes wrong in his dealings with literature, it is because he judges literature by too limited an application of these principles. When he praises literature, it is chiefly because of its powers of factual representation, its powers of discovery—"Not I but the poets," he said, "discovered the unconscious." When he denigrates literature (by implication), it is by speaking of its mere hedonism, of its being an escape from reality, a substitute-gratification, a daydream, an anodyne. Some years ago I dealt as sternly as I could with the errors of these formulations of Freud's, and so now perhaps I am privileged to lighten the burden of reprobation they have had to bear and to take note of a certain rightness and usefulness they have.

Freud is scarcely unique in conceiving of literature in terms of the opposition between reality and pleasure. This conception is endemic in literary criticism itself since at least the time of Plato, and often in a very simple form. It was usually in a very simple form that the opposition was made in the nineteenth century. We have but to read the young Yeats and to observe his passion against fact and the literature of fact, and his avowed preference for the literature of dream, to see how established in the thought of the time was the opposition between the pleasure principle and the principle of reality.

Nowadays literary criticism tends to be restive under the opposition, which it takes to be a covert denial of the autonomy of literature, a way of judging literature by the categories of science. But the poets themselves have always accepted the opposition and still do. They accept the commission to represent something called reality, which lies outside of literature, and which they think of as either antagonistic to the dream of pleasure, or as standing beyond pleasure and, as it were, led to and served by pleasure. Sometimes, at the behest of reality, they question and even reprobate their hedonistic dreams. Wordsworth blames himself for having "lived in a dream," for having failed to represent to himself the painful adversity of the world. Keats denounces himself for his membership in the "tribe" of mere dreaming poets, who are so much less than "those to whom the miseries of the world / Are misery, and will not let them rest."

> What benefit canst thou do, or all thy tribe,
> To the great world? Thou art a dreaming thing,
> A fever of thyself—think of the Earth . . .

Yet with the dream of pleasure, or with the actuality of pleasure, the poets always keep in touch. Keats's whole mental life was an effort to demonstrate the continuity between pleasure and reality. Wordsworth speaks of the principle of pleasure—the phrase is his—as constituting the "naked and native dignity of man." He says, moreover, that it is the principle by which man not only "feels, and lives, and moves," but also "knows": the principle of pleasure is for Wordsworth the very ground of the principle of reality, and so of course it is for Freud, even though he seems to maintain the irreconcilability of the two principles. And the mature Yeats, in that famous sentence of his, which is as Freudian in its tendency as it is Wordsworthian, tells us that, "In dreams begins responsibility." He bases the developed moral life on the autonomy of the youthful hedonistic phantasies.

"Beauty is truth, truth beauty," said Keats, and generations of critics have been at pains to tell us that the equations are false. They forget what meaning we are required to assign to the two predications by reason of the fact that Keats utters them in the context of a passionate meditation on four great facts of human existence—love, death, art, and the relation that exists among these. When Keats says that beauty is truth, he is saying that the pleasure principle is at the root of existence, and of knowledge, and of the moral life. When he says that truth is beauty, he is putting in two words his enormously complex belief that the self can so develop that it may, in the intensity of art or meditation, perceive even very painful facts with a kind of pleasure, for it is one of the striking things about Keats that he represents so boldly and accurately the development of the self, and that, when he speaks of pleasure, he may mean—to use a language not his—sometimes the pleasure of the id, sometimes the pleasure of the ego, and sometimes the pleasure of the super-ego.

Keats's mind was profoundly engaged by the paradox of the literary genre of tragedy, which must always puzzle us because it seems to propose to the self a gratification in regarding its own extinction. Very eminent psychoanalysts, continuators of Freud's science who would perhaps differ with him on no other point, do differ with him on the point of his having conceived a tendency of the self by which it acquiesces in and even desires its own end. Whether or not Freud's formulations of the death instinct stand up under scientific inquiry, I of course cannot venture to say. But certainly they confirm our sense of Freud's oneness with the tradition of literature. For literature has always recorded an impulse of the self to find affirmation even in its own extinction, even *by* its own extinction. If we read the great scene of the death of Oedipus at Colonus, we have little trouble, I think, in at least suspending our disbelief in Freud's idea. We do so the more willingly because the impulse to death is, in this magnificent moment, expressed and exemplified by the most passionate of men, the man in whom the energy of will and intellect was greatest, the man, too, who at the moment of his desire for death speaks of his extraordinary power of love. It is possible to argue that Oedipus does not in fact go to his death but to his apotheosis. It is possible, too, to say that when the poets speak of the desire for death or the happy acquiescence in death, they do not really mean death at all but apotheosis, or Nirvana, or what Yeats imagined, the existence "out of nature," in the "artifice of eternity." It is possible to say that something of this sort is really what Freud meant. But the poets call it death; it has much of the aspect of death; and when we take into account the age-old impulse of highly developed spirits to incorporate the idea of death into the experience of life, even to make death the criterion of life, we are hard put to it to say that the assertion of the death instinct is nothing but a pathology, that it is not the effort of finely tempered minds to affirm the self in an ultimate confrontation of reality.

There is yet another theme with which literature and Freud have an equal preoccupation. It is again a theme of opposition, cognate with the opposition between pleasure and reality—the theme of the opposition between love and power. That literature does conceive love and power as being in opposition is obvious enough from the frequency with which it presents the hero as both lover and warrior, the interest of his situation being that he finds it very hard to reconcile his desire for love and his desire for power. The theme has preoccupied not only the dramatic poets and the novelists but the lyric poets too—it was a lyric poet who put so large a part of the matter in a nutshell: "I could not love thee (Deare) so much, / Lov'd I not Honour more," for the power I speak of is not gross, cruel power (although, in the context, this cannot be far from our minds) but rather, in its ideal conception, what is represented by the word honor: it is the power of cultural achievement, or of cultural commitment. As such, it was seen by Freud as pre-eminently a masculine problem. "The masculine character, the ability to dare and endure, to know and not to fear reality, to look the world in the face and take it for what it is,... this is what I want to preserve." It is not Freud I am quoting but one of Henry James's heroes, an American; but Basil Ransom of *The Bostonians* says very well what Freud meant. And Freud's concern for the preservation of what James calls "the masculine character," which, like James, Freud conceived to be under attack, has been made a point in the reproach directed at Freud that he displayed a masculine chauvinism, and, what is more, that, for all his overt preoccupation with love, he was yet more preoccupied with power, with aggression and personal force, or, at the best, with achievement. This contributes to a tendency which is to be observed of recent years, the tendency to represent Freud as really anaesthetic to love and as in some way antagonistic to it. We all know how it has been said of Freud that he has made love out to be nothing but a reaction-formation against the most selfish and hostile impulses. And so strange are the surprises of the movement of thought that Freud, once attacked for the extravagance of his sexual emphasis, is now, by people of no little seriousness, said to be puritanical in his view of sexuality, surrendering to civilization and to achievement in civilization far more of impulse than there was any need to surrender.

This is not a matter that can be argued here. I should like only to turn again to literature and to observe that the tendency of literature, when once it has represented the opposition between love and power, is to conceive of love as a principle of order for the self, even as a discipline, and as itself a power, a civic and civilizing power. Oedipus, that angry and violent man who pauses in his dying to set the word *love* at the very heart of experience, saying of himself, as Yeats translates the speech, "No living man has loved as I have loved," becomes the guardian genius of the Athenian civic life. William Blake, who envisaged life in a way that Freud would have easily understood, calls in a great voice, "Bring me my bow of burning gold! Bring me my arrows of desire. Bring me my spear!..." What does he want this libidinal armament for? Why, that he "may build Jerusalem in England's green and pleasant land." And in his great poem on the death of Freud, W. H. Auden speaks of the grief both of "anarchic Aphrodite" and of "Eros, builder of cities."

Freud himself had as a personal trait a very large measure of the love of honor. He was personally much concerned with cultural commitment and achievement. And he loved fame.

To some it may be surprising and even dismaying that I should speak of Freud's love of fame. It may seem that it does no credit to Freud to speak of his love of fame, that it is inappropriate that I should do so on an occasion like this one, and that it is incongruous to mention it in conjunction with his cultural commitment. For in our culture the love of fame is not considered a virtue, or even an attractive trait of the personality. We are likely to confuse it with the love of publicity, and thus to be confirmed in our feeling that it is not a worthy motive of intellectual commitment. It is, I believe, considered particularly unbecoming in a scientist. But it is a trait which confirms our sense of Freud's personal connection with the tradition of literature, and my mention of it is meant as praise. Traditionally the love of fame has characterized two highly regarded professions, that of arms and that of letters. The soldier, however, is no longer supposed to desire fame. And even the poet, although I think we license him to entertain the phantasy of his immortal renown, no longer praises fame or says he wants it, as once he thought it very proper to do. Dante desired above all earthly things to be famous as a poet. Shakespeare believed implicitly in the permanence of his fame. Milton calls the love of fame "that last infirmity of noble mind," but he thus connects it with mind; and he speaks of it as an ally of the reality principle:

> Fame is the spur that the *clear* spirit doth raise
> To scorn delights and live laborious days.

Well, there can be no doubt that fame was the spur to Freud's clear spirit, to his desire to make clear what was darkly seen. As a student he stood in the great Aula of the University of Vienna, where were set up the busts of the famous men of the University, and he dreamed of the day when he should be similarly honored. He knew exactly what inscription he wanted on the pedestal, a line from *Oedipus Tyrannus*, "Who divined the riddle of the Sphinx and was a man most mighty"—the story is told by his biographer that he turned pale, as if he had seen a ghost, when, on his fiftieth birthday, he was presented by his friends and admirers with a medallion on which these very words were inscribed.

And if we ask what moves the poets to their love of fame, what made the dying Keats say in despair, "Here lies one whose name is writ in water," and then again in hope, "I shall be among the English poets," the answer is not so very difficult to come by. The poets' idea of fame is the intense expression of the sense of the self, of the self defined by the thing it makes, which is conceived to be everlasting precisely because it was once a new thing, a thing added to the spirit of man.

My attempt to suggest the connection of Freud's thought with the tradition of literature must end here. I know how inadequate is the comparison I have drawn, and how merely random must seem the points of similarity I have chosen. Yet perhaps I have said enough to lead you to recall, possibly in a new way, what you have always known, that the connection between Freud and literature is of an integral kind. And perhaps too I have said enough to lead you to infer that the connection is of more than curious interest, that it is, as I believe it to be, of practical interest.

I have undertaken to speak of Freud in relation to our culture, and, at that, in relation to a crisis in our culture. If I have given this much time to speaking first of Freud in relation to literature, that is because I believe that the complex accuracy of Freud's view of culture may best be spoken of in terms of his affinity with the tradition of literary humanism.

Literature offers itself to our understanding in many ways. Of these not the least important is that which takes literature to be an intellectual discipline having to do with appearance and reality, with truth. The truth we especially expect literature to convey to us by its multifarious mode of communication is the truth of the self, and also the truth about the self, about the conditions of its existence, its survival, its development. For literature, as for Freud, the self is the first prime object of attention and solicitude. The culture in which the self has its existence is a matter of the liveliest curiosity, but in a secondary way, as an essential condition of

the self, as a chief object of the self's energies, or as represent-
ing the aggregation of selves. But for literature, as for Freud,
the test of the culture is always the individual self, not the
other way around. The function of literature, through all its
mutations, has been to make us aware of the particularity of
selves, and the high authority of the self in its quarrel with its
society and its culture. Literature is in that sense subversive.
This is not to say that the general culture does not have its
own kind of awareness of the self. It does; it must—and when
we judge a culture we inevitably adduce the way it conceives
of the self, the value and honor it gives to the self. But it can
sometimes happen that a culture intent upon giving the very
highest value and honor to the selves that comprise it can
proceed on its generous enterprise without an accurate
awareness of what the self is, or what it may be. Such a loss
of accurate knowledge about the self it is possible to observe
in our own culture at this time. It is, I believe, a very generous culture, and in its conscious thought it sets great store
by the conditions of life which are manifestly appropriate
to the self, the conditions of freedom and respect. Yet it
would seem that this generosity of intention does not pre-
clude a misapprehension of the nature of the self, and of the
right relation of the self to the culture. This progressive de-

terioration of accurate knowledge of the self and of the right relation between the self and the culture constitutes what I am calling a crisis in our culture. To the theories and formulas which serve to rationalize this deterioration Freud's thought about the self and the culture stands as a challenge and a controversion. It is this challenge and controversion that I shall go on to speak of.

The idea of culture, in the modern sense of the word, is a relatively new idea. It represents a way of thinking about our life in society which developed concommitantly with certain new ways of conceiving of the self. Indeed, our modern idea of culture may be thought of as a new sort of selfhood bestowed upon the whole of society. The idea of society as a person is not new, but there is much that is new about the kind of personalization of society which began to be made some two hundred years ago. Society, in this new selfhood, is thought of as having a certain organic unity, an autonomous character and personality which it expresses in everything it does; it is conceived to have a *style*, which is manifest not only in its conscious, intentional activities, in its architecture, its philosophy, and so on, but also in its unconscious activities, in its unexpressed assumptions—the unconscious of society may be said to have been imagined before the unconscious of the individual. And in the degree that society was personalized by the concept of culture, the individual was seen to be far more deeply implicated in society than ever before. This is not an idea which is confined to the historian or to the social scientists; it is an idea which is at work in the mind of every literate and conscious person as he thinks of his life and estimates the chances of his living well in the world. At some point in the history of the West—let us say, for convenience, at the time of Rousseau—men began to think of their fates as being lived out not in relation to God, or to the individual persons who are their neighbors, or to material circumstance, but to the ideas and assumptions and manners of a large social totality. The evidence of this is to be found in our literature, in its preoccupation with newly discovered alien cultures which, in one regard or another, serve to criticize our own. Walter Scott could not have delighted the world with his representation in *Waverley* of the loyalty, sincerity, and simplicity of the Highland clans had not the world learned to think of life in terms of culture, had it not learned to wonder whether some inscrutable bad principle in its present culture was not making it impossible for all men to be as loyal and sincere and simple as they should be.

In the dissemination of the idea of culture, Freud has no doubt had a chief part. The status of Freud's actual formulations about culture is now somewhat ambiguous. We often hear it said that Freud's theories of culture are inadequate. It seems to me, in my ignorance of the refinements of cultural theory, that this is often said by writers on the subject just before they make use of some one of Freud's ideas about culture. But whatever we may conclude about the intellectual value of Freud's formulations, we cannot fail to know that it was Freud who made the idea of culture real for a great many of us. Whatever he may mean to the people who deal professionally with the idea of culture—and in point of fact he means a great deal—for the layman Freud is likely to be the chief proponent of the whole cultural concept. It was he who made it apparent to us how entirely implicated in culture we all are. By what he said or suggested of the depth and subtlety of the influence of the family upon the individual, he made plain how the culture suffuses the remotest parts of the individual mind, being taken in almost literally with the mother's milk. His psychology involves culture in its very essence—it tells us that the surrogates of culture are established in the mind itself, that the development of the individual mind recapitulates the development of culture.

Generally speaking, the word "culture" is used in an honorific sense. When we look at a people in the degree of abstraction which the idea of culture implies, we cannot but be touched and impressed by what we see, we cannot help being awed by something mysterious at work, some creative power which seems to transcend any particular act or habit or quality that may be observed. To make a coherent life, to confront the terrors of the inner and the outer world, to establish the ritual and art, the pieties and duties which make possible the life of the group and the individual—these are culture, and to contemplate these efforts of culture is inevitably moving. And, indeed, without this sympathy and admiration a culture is a closed book to the student, for the scientific attitude requisite for the study of cultures is based on a very lively subjectivity. It is not merely that the student of culture must make a willing suspension of disbelief in the assumptions of cultures other than his own; he must go even further and feel that the culture he has under examination is somehow justified, that it is as it should be.

This methodological sympathy, as we might call it, developed into a kind of principle of cultural autonomy, according to which cultures were to be thought of as self-contained systems not open to criticism from without; and this principle was taken from the anthropologists by certain psychoanalysts. In this view a culture became a kind of absolute. The culture was not to be judged "bad" or "neurotic"; it was the individual who was to be judged by the criteria of the culture. This view, I believe, no longer obtains in its old force. We are no longer forbidden to judge cultures adversely; we may now speak of them as inadequate cultures, even as downright neurotic cultures. And yet the feeling for the absoluteness of culture still persists. It may best be observed in our responses to the cultures we think of as having a "folk" character and in our tendency to suppose that when an individual is at one with a culture of this sort he is in a happy and desirable state of existence. This will suggest the unconscious use we make of the idea of culture: we take it to be a useful and powerful support to the idea of *community*, for what we respond to in a folk culture is what we see, or seem to see, of the unity and coherence of its individual members, the absence of conflict, the sense of the wholeness of the group.

But Freud's attitude to culture is different from this. For him, too, there is an honorific tonality in the use of the word. But at the same time, as we cannot fail to hear, there is in what he says about culture an unfailing note of exasperation and resistance. Freud's relation to culture must be described as an ambivalent one.

Recently, in another connection, I spoke of the modern self as characterized by its intense and adverse imagination of the culture in which it had its being, and by certain powers of indignant perception which, turned upon the unconscious portions of culture, have made it accessible to conscious thought. Freud's view of culture is marked by this *adverse* awareness, by this indignant perception. He does indeed see the self as formed by its culture. But he also sees the self as set against the culture, struggling against it, having been from the first reluctant to enter it. Freud would have understood what Hegel meant by speaking of the "*terrible* principle of culture." This resistance, this tragic regret over the necessary involvement with culture, is obviously not the sole or even the dominant element in Freud's thought on the subject. Freud was, as he said of himself, a conservative, a conserving, mind. The aim of all his effort is the service of culture—he speaks of the work of psychoanalysis as "the draining of the Zuyder Zee," the building of the dyke, the seeing to it that where id was ego should be. Yet at the same time his adverse attitude to culture is very strong, his indignation is very intense.

It can of course be said that the indignation which an individual directs upon his culture is itself culturally conditioned. Culture may be thought of as Kismet—we flee from Bokhara to escape its decrees, only to fulfill them in Samara. Yet the illusion, if that is what it be, of separateness from one's culture has an effect upon conduct, and upon culture, which is as decisive as the effects of the illusion of free will. For Freud this separateness was a necessary belief. He needed to believe that there was some point at which it was possible to stand beyond the reach of culture. Perhaps his formulation of the death-instinct is to be interpreted as the expression of this need. "Death destroys a man," says E. M. Forster, "but the idea of death saves him." Saves him from what? From the entire submission of himself—of his self—to life in culture.

At this point you will perhaps be wondering why I said that Freud so greatly influenced our present-day idea of culture, for certainly this aspect of Freud's thought—his resistance to culture—is not reflected in the thought of our present-day, educated, enlightened, progressive middle class. That class sets so much store by the idea of man in culture because, as I say, it sets so much store (and rightly) by the idea of man in community. The two ideas are not the same. But the idea of man-in-culture provides, as it were, the metaphysic, the mystique, of our ideas of man-in-community. It gives us a way of speaking more profoundly about community, for talking about souls, about destiny, about the ground and sanctions of morality; it is our way of talking about fate, free will, and immortality. It is our way of coming close to the idea of Providence. I of course do not mean that we of the educated, enlightened, progressive middle class do not criticize our culture as it actually is. Indeed, nothing is more characteristic of this class than its readiness to observe certain obvious failings and inadequacies of its cultural situation. Yet in every criticism that we utter, we express our belief that man can be truly himself and fully human only if he is in accord with his cultural environment, and, also, only if the cultural environment is in accord with the best tendencies in himself. This idea is not specifically a Freudian idea. It is the idea, or the assumption, on which the tradition of humane liberal thought has gone about its business for two centuries. But although it was not in the first instance derived from Freud, it is confirmed by the tendency of certain Freudian ideas. And it may be said to constitute the ground of the Freudianism of the American educated middle class, expressed in that class's theories of education, child-rearing, morality, and social action.

But if we speak of the Freudianism of the American educated middle class, we must also speak of the anti-Freudianism of the American educated middle class. An ambivalent attitude toward Freudianism is perhaps inevitable and may-be even healthy. But I do not have in mind what might be called the normal ambivalence of response to Freud's ideas. Rather, I speak of the particular resentment—for such it can be called—of Freud's theories of the self in its relation to culture. What I have described of Freud's tragic sense of culture, of his apparent wish to establish the self beyond the reach of culture, will suggest the ground for this hostility. For the fact is that Freud challenges our sense of how the self relates to culture and of how it should relate to culture. He shakes us most uncomfortably in those very ideas which we believe we have learned from him.

There was recently held a conference of psychiatrists for the purpose of considering the effect upon the psychic health of the nation of a certain cultural tendency of obvious importance, the tendency represented by requiring oaths of loyalty, by putting people under surveillance, by inquiring into the ideas and attitudes and pasts and associations of men and women holding civic positions.[1] This tendency of suspiciousness and repressiveness is no doubt latent in all cultures; in American culture it has periodically made itself manifest in dramatic ways; its most recent manifestation we came to call McCarthyism, and it was this that the psychiatric conference was met to consider as a factor in the psychic health of the nation. The consensus at the conference was that the tendency of repressiveness must inevitably have a bad effect upon our national psychic health. It was not merely said that individuals would be made the prey of intense anxiety. The harm was said to be of a far deeper kind and likely to be perpetuated in the culture. For the ego is the aspect of the mind that deals with the object-world, and one of its important functions is the pleasurable entertainment of the idea of adventure. But if part of the object-world is closed off by interdiction, and if the impulse to adventure is checked by a restrictive culture, the free functioning of the ego is impaired. No less subject to injury is the super-ego— it was said at the conference that "a mature super-ego can optimally develop only in a free and democratic society."

---

[1]"Considerations Regarding the Loyalty Oath as a Manifestation of Current Social Tension and Anxiety: A Statement Formulated by the Committee on Social Issues of the Group for the Advancement of Psychiatry and a Panel Discussion." G.A.P. Symposium No. 1, Topeka, Kansas, October 1954.

Now obviously there is much in this that no one will disagree with. What the conference says in the language of psychiatry, we all say in our own language. If you enslave a man, he will develop the psychology of a slave. If you exclude a man from free access to the benefits of society, his human quality will be materially diminished. All men of good intention are likely to say something of this kind as they think of social betterment.

And yet if we look critically at these ideas, they will be seen not to go so far along the way to truth as at first we think. What, to take a relevant example, was the cultural and political situation in which Freud's thought developed, and his ego and his super-ego too? Dr. Jones tells us something about this in the first volume of his biography of Freud, but I shall draw my answer from the report of an American writer whom Freud particularly admired. Mark Twain lived in Vienna at the time Freud was formulating his theory of psychoanalysis; he attended many of the sessions of the Parliament of 1897 and he described some of them. One event, which especially horrified him, was the Parliament's surrender of its own authority, for it invited a militarized police force to march into the House itself to remove certain unruly members. Mark Twain certainly had no high opinion of the manners of American legislators, but he was appalled by what he observed in the Viennese Parliament, the show of personal violence, the personal invective of the rudest and most obscene sort. "As to the make-up of the House itself," he said, "it is this: the deputies come from all the walks of life and from all the grades of society. There are princes, counts, barons, priests, mechanics, laborers, lawyers, physicians, professors, merchants, bankers, shopkeepers. They are religious men, they are earnest, sincere, devoted, and they hate the Jews." This was the one point of unity in a Parliament which was the battleground of the fiercest nationalistic and cultural jealousies. And the weakness of Parliament meant the strength of the monarchical government, which ruled by police methods; censorship was in force, and only inefficiency kept it from being something graver than a nuisance.

No one, of course, will conclude that Freud lived under oppression in the society of his Vienna. Still, it was anything but a free and democratic society as the conference of psychiatrists, or most of us, would define a free and democratic society, and Freud was not an enfranchised citizen of it until his middle years. His having been reared in such a society surely goes far to explain why some of his views of culture are tragic or skeptical, and very far toward explaining why he conceived of the self as standing in opposition to the general culture. But the cultural circumstance in which he was reared did not, so far as I can make out, impair the functioning of his ego or his super-ego.

Why did it not? Well, certain things in his particular cultural situation intervened between him and the influence of his society. His family situation, for one thing: the family is the conduit of cultural influences, but it is also a bulwark against cultural influences. His ethnic situation for another thing: he was a Jew, and enough of the Jewish sub-culture reached him to make a countervailing force against the general culture. Then his education: who can say what part in self-respect, in the ability to move to a point beyond the reach of the surrounding dominant culture, has been played by the old classical education, with its image of *the other culture,* the ideal culture, that wonderful imagined culture of the ancient world which no one but schoolboys, schoolmasters, scholars, and poets believed in? The schoolboy who kept his diary in Greek, as Freud did, was not submitting his ego or his super-ego to the debilitating influences of a restrictive society. Then the culture of another nation intervened between him and what was bad in his own culture:

Freud's early love of England must be counted among his defenses. Then he found strength in certain aspects of his own culture, bad as it may have been by our standards of freedom and democracy: he loved the language and thus made it his friend, and he loved science.

And then beyond these cultural interpositions there was his sense of himself as a biological fact. This sense of himself as a biological fact was of course supported and confirmed by the various accidents of Freud's cultural fate, but it was, to begin with, a *given*, a *donnée*—a gift. It was a particular quantity and a particular quality of human energy, and its name was Sigmund Freud.

The place of biology in Freud's system of thought has often been commented on, and generally adversely. It is often spoken of as if it represents a reactionary part of Freud's thought. The argument takes this form: if we think of a man as being conditioned not so much by biology as by culture, we can the more easily envisage a beneficent manipulation of his condition; if we keep our eyes fixed upon the wide differences among cultures which may be observed, and if we repudiate Freud's naive belief that there is a human *given* in all persons and all cultures, then we are indeed encouraged to think that we can do what we wish with ourselves, with mankind—there is no beneficent mutation of culture, there is no revision of the nature of man, that we cannot hope to bring about.

Now Freud may be right or he may be wrong in the place he gives to biology in human fate, but I think we must stop to consider whether this emphasis on biology, whether correct or incorrect, is not so far from being a reactionary idea that it is actually a liberating idea. It proposes to us that culture is not all-powerful. It suggests that there is a residue of human quality beyond the reach of cultural control, and that this residue of human quality, elemental as it may be, serves to bring culture itself under criticism and keeps it from being absolute.

This consideration is, I believe, of great importance to us at this moment in our history. The argument I made from Freud's own cultural situation in boyhood was, as I know, in some degree unfair, for the society of Vienna, although certainly not what we would call free and democratic, was apparently such a mess of a society that one might, without difficulty, escape whatever bad intentions it had; and its tolerance of mess may lead us to conclude that it had certain genial intentions of freedom. Nowadays, however, societies are less likely to be messes; they are likely to be all too efficient, whether by coerciveness or seductiveness. In a society like ours, which, despite some appearances to the contrary, tends to be seductive rather than coercive, the individual's old defenses against the domination of the culture become weaker and weaker. The influence of the family deteriorates and is replaced by the influence of the school. The small separatist group set apart by religious or ethnic difference loses its authority, or uses what authority it has to support the general culture. The image of what I have called *the other culture,* the idealized past of some other nation, Greece, or Rome, or England, is dismissed from education at the behest of the pedagogic sense of reality—it is worth noting that, for perhaps the first time in history, the pedagogue is believed to have a sense of reality. And we have come to understand that it is not a low Philistine impulse that leads us to scrutinize with anxiety our children's success in their social life; it is rather a frank, free, generous, democratic, progressive awareness of the charms of Group-Living, an engaging trust—only the least little bit ironic, and the irony is easily suppressed—of the natural happiness of man-in-culture, or child-in-culture, so long as that culture is not overtly hostile.

One does not need to have a very profound quarrel with

American culture to feel uneasy because our defenses against it, our modes of escape from it, are becoming less and less adequate. One may even have a very lively admiration for American culture, as I do, and yet feel that this defenselessness of the self against its culture is cause for alarm.

Our culture is in process of revision, and of revision in a very good and right direction, in the direction of greater openness, greater socialization, greater cooperativeness, greater reasonableness. There are, to be sure, tendencies to be observed which go counter to this one, but they are not, I believe, so momentous as the development of the tendency toward social peace. It must always seem ill-natured to raise any question at all about this tendency. It goes against the grain to do so. Yet at least one question has already been raised within, as it were, the ranks of the good, and we may as well take advantage of this opportunity to be critical without being disagreeable. I said that now, perhaps for the first time in history, the pedagogue is presumed to have a sense of reality; the idea of a pedagogic sense of reality is not thought of as a contradiction in terms. That is because the dominant pedagogic theory of our time is the expression of the ideal of community by which the educated American middle class sets such store. Yet at the moment a great many of us have come to feel that our ideal of community as it expresses itself in the theory and practice of pedagogy has had a very bad effect on our educational system.

We carefully dissociate ourselves from the reactionary elements that attack modern modes of education, and still we come more and more to believe that the elaborate ideology of "integration with the group," of "cooperation," of "whole development," or "social studies" and "communication arts" is in effect the highly intellectualized rationalization of some deep-seated anti-intellectualism. We know that the conscious intention of this pedagogy is to foster equality and democracy and good will, but we begin to perceive that it is hostile to distinction, and to mind, and to accuracy of thought, and at a moment in our history when distinction, and mind, and accuracy of thought were never more needed. *false reason*

Devoted as this pedagogy is to the ideal of integrating the self with society and culture, we come increasingly to believe that the self it conceives is far from being what we hope the self may be.

But it is always easy to mock pedagogical theory. Let us try something harder. The American educated middle class is firm in its admiration of non-conformity and dissent. The right to be non-conformist, the right to dissent, is part of our conception of community. Everybody says so: in the weekly, monthly, quarterly magazines and in *The New York Times*, at the cocktail party, at the conference of psychiatrists, at the conference of teachers. How good this is, and how right! And yet, when we examine the content of our idea of non-conformity, we must be dismayed at the smallness of the concrete actuality this very large idea contains. The rhetoric is as sincere as it is capacious, yet we must sometimes wonder whether what is being praised and defended is anything more than the right to have had some sympathetic connection with Communism ten or twenty years ago. Men of principle have opposed reactionary tendencies in our society and some have taken risks in their opposition, but for most of us our settled antagonism to that instance of reactionary tendency we call McCarthyism is simply the badge of our class. Our imagination of dissent from our culture can scarcely go beyond this. We cannot really imagine non-conformity at all, not in art, not in moral or social theory, certainly not in the personal life—it is probably true that there never was a culture which required so entire an eradication of personal differentiation, so bland a uniformity of manner. Admiring non-conformity and loving community, we have decided that we are all non-conformists together. We assert the right of our egos to court

cf Torqueville

adventure without danger and of our super-egos to be con-
scientious without undue strain. We make, I think, what is
in many ways a very attractive culture, but we really cannot
imagine what it means to take an intellectual chance, or to
make an intellectual mistake, or to have a real intellectual
difference. You have but to read our novels to understand
that we have a growing sense of the cooperative virtues and
a diminishing sense of the self that cooperates. We have, as
a class, agreed on the right amount of disaffected criticism,
or anger, that we shall direct against our culture, and we have
agreed upon the aspects of our culture which are to be the
objects of our criticism and anger. Having determined the
inoculating dose that assures the health of our self-respect,
we are likely to be thrown into a panic by anyone who
tampers with it—we fear all modulating ideas as if they were
the negation of the reality of our existence.

We must, I think, recognize how open and available to
the general culture the individual has become, how little pro-
tected he is by countervailing cultural forces, how unified and
demanding our free culture has become. And if we do recognize this, we can begin to see why we may think of Freud's
emphasis on biology as being a liberating idea. It is a resistance to and a modification of the cultural omnipotence. We

reflect that somewhere in the child, somewhere in the adult, there is a hard, irreducible, stubborn core of biological urgency, and biological necessity, and biological *reason,* which culture cannot reach and which reserves the right, which sooner or later it will exercise, to judge the culture and resist and revise it. It seems to me that whenever we become aware of how entirely we are involved in our culture and how entirely controlled by it we believe ourselves to be, destined and fated and foreordained by it, there must come to us a certain sense of liberation when we remember our biological selves. In her Anniversary Lecture of 1954, Anna Freud spoke of what she called the period of optimism in the psychoanalytical thought about the rearing of children, a period when, as she says, "almost the whole blame for the neurotic development of the child was laid on parental actions" and when "it was hoped that the modification of these parental attitudes would do away with infantile anxiety and, consequently, abolish the infantile neuroses." And Miss Freud went on to speak of the following "period of pessimism, when the origin of neurosis was recognized to be due not to environmental influences but to inevitable factors of various kinds." Pessimistic this new period of psychoanalytical thought may be; yet when we think of the growing power of culture to control us by seduction or coercion, we must be glad and not sorry that some part of our fate comes from outside the culture.

We must not permit ourselves to be at the mercy of the terrible pendulum of thought and begin now to discredit all that we have learned about cultural influence or conclude that parents have been suddenly relieved of all responsibility for their children's psychic destinies. Yet this new emphasis, of which Miss Freud speaks, upon the non-cultural part of our destiny may well serve to renovate and freshen our mode of thinking about ourselves.

The interaction of biology and culture in the fate of man is not a matter which we have yet begun to understand. Up to now, entranced by all that the idea of culture and the study of culture can tell us about the nature of man, we have been inclined to assign to culture an almost exclusive part in man's fate. If the culture goes awry, we say, inevitably the individual goes awry—his ego and his super-ego suffer serious impairment. But history does not always support this view. Sometimes it does, but not always. It is sometimes to be observed that a whole people will degenerate because of a drastic change in its economic and political and thus of its cultural situation. But then too, it sometimes happens that a people living under imposed conditions of a very bad kind, the opposite of the conditions of that free and democratic society which the ego and the super-ego are said to need for health and maturity, living, indeed, under persecution, will develop egos and super-egos of an amazing health and strength. Whether also of maturity I will not venture to say, for maturity is a difficult word to comprehend and it is very difficult, when once we comprehend it, to carry its meaning from one culture to another: but strength and health they certainly have, enough to make for survival on a high cultural level. They have their psychic casualties, their psychic scars are manifest, but they survive in sufficient dignity. And if we ask why they thus survived, the answer may be that they conceived of their egos and super-egos as not being culturally conditioned and dependent but as being virtually biological facts, and immutable. And often they put this conception of their psyches to the ultimate biological test—they died for the immutability of their egos and super-egos.

What, to shift our ground from the group to the individuals, made it possible for a Giordano Bruno, or a Socrates, or any other martyr of the intellect, to face his death? It was not, I think, that a free and democratic society had successfully nurtured the maturity of his super-ego. How very strange is the super-ego! For we say of it that it is the surrogate of society, or of the culture, but one of its functions seems to be to lead us to imagine that there is a sanction beyond the culture, that there is a place from which the culture may be judged and rejected. It often happens that culture is very grateful for being so judged and rejected, that it gives the highest reminiscent honors to those who have escaped it. But we make it that much harder to escape the culture, we cut off the possibility of those triumphs of the mind that are won in the face of culture, if we impose the idea of a self that is wholly dependent upon the culture for its energy and health.

"Suppose," I heard a student on my own campus say the other day, "Suppose a man is paranoid—that is, he thinks he is right and other people are wrong." He did not really, or he did not wholly, mean what he said—had he been questioned, he would have owned to a lively and reasoned admiration for the long tradition of the men who thought they were right and everybody else was wrong, he would have happily admitted that this isolation in belief was not only a sign of insanity. But at the moment at which he made his utterance he was speaking with the voice of the tendency of his culture. He was not one of the group of my own students who, a short time ago, read with me Freud's *Civilization and Its Discontents,* but he was kin to them, for they told me that Freud had presented a paranoid version of the relation of the self to culture: he conceived of the self submitting to culture and being yet in opposition to it; he conceived of the self as being not wholly continuous with culture, as being not wholly created by culture, as maintaining a standing quarrel with its great benefactor.

I need scarcely remind you that in respect of this "paranoia" Freud is quite at one with literature. In its essence literature is concerned with the self; and the particular concern of the literature of the last two centuries has been with the self in its standing quarrel with culture. We cannot mention the name of any great writer of the modern period whose work has not in some way, and usually in a passionate and explicit way, insisted on this quarrel, who has not expressed the bitterness of his discontent with civilization, who has not said that the self made greater legitimate demands than any culture could hope to satisfy. This intense conviction of the existence of the self apart from culture is, as culture well knows, its noblest and most generous achievement. At the present moment it must be thought of as a liberating idea without which our developing ideal of community is bound to defeat itself. We can speak no greater praise of Freud than to say that he placed this idea at the very center of his thought.